portraits

of love

THE STONEWALL INN BOOK SERIES:

THE NAME OF LOVE: *Classic Gay Love Poems,*
edited by Michael Lassell

THE KEY TO EVERYTHING: *Classic Lesbian Love Poems,*
edited by Gerry Gomez Pearlberg

IN YOUR EYES: *Quotations on Gay Love,*
edited by Richard M. Derus

A DELICATE FIRE: *Quotations on Lesbian Love,*
edited by Liz Tracey

PORTRAITS OF LOVE: *Lesbians Writing About Love,*
edited by Susan Fox Rogers
and Linda Smukler

TWO HEARTS DESIRE: *Gay Couples on Their Love,*
edited by Michael Lassell and Lawrence Schimel

EDITED BY
Susan Fox Rogers and
Linda Smukler

portraits
—————
of love

*Lesbians Writing*
*About Love*

A STONEWALL INN BOOK
ST. MARTIN'S PRESS ❧ NEW YORK

Design by Songhee Kim

Library of Congress Cataloging-in-Publication Data

Portraits of love : writings by lesbian couples / edited by
    Susan Fox Rogers and Linda Smukler. — 1st ed.
        p.   cm.
    ISBN 0-312-15192-6
    1. Lesbians' writings, American.   2. Lesbian cou-
ples—Literary collections.   3. Lesbians—Literary collections.   I. Rogers, Susan Fox.   II. Smukler, Linda.
PS509.L47P67   1997
810.8'09206643—dc20                                    96-42519
                                                            CIP

First Edition: February 1997

10   9   8   7   6   5   4   3   2   1

"Love, Maybe" from *Undersong: Chosen Poems Old and New* © 1992, 1973 by Audre Lorde. W. W. Norton, Inc., New York. Reprinted by permission of the publisher.

(*continued on page 83*)

*SR: for LS*
*LS: for SR*
*of course*

———————————————

*Thanks to Keith Kahla, for all of this, Mikel Wadewitz for keeping everything moving. Babka, Max, and Smudge for the nudges. The Chicago El for running on time. Our boy partners, Lawrence and Michael. And everyone who sent us their portraits.*

# Contents

## I. MAY 26, 1996: MEMORIAL DAY

Susan: Shall we write our introduction? We've done just about everything else together.

Linda: I love your fingernail skin  and the back of your knuckles  it astounds me that you are so willing to go along with it all  except that we were supposed to go on a hike today  we planted roses instead then it got too late and I had reservations so instead we are sitting here and writing for this book  now what?

We should go for a walk, of course. A walk up a mountain, a walk down the street, a walk in the park. Hand in hand, arm in arm, we do this so easily, unself-consciously in these odd little towns near where we call home.

Up and down the streets of Chatham  then through the herb fair  could so many heterosexuals exist in the same place at the same time? don't think so  and yet it's where our home happens to be and then again we learned about bedstraw and cattail flour

# Introduction

Imagine round baby cat  I put that on the refrigerator a month ago  and now there are two round baby cats jumping around the living room  I now love the color of our refrigerator  mustard-yellow or according to G.E.  Harvest Gold

You asked me the color of that refrigerator when you know that I am color—not blind—but indifferent. You are the one who wanted blue tiles on the kitchen countertop, and sahara on the floor. I could easily have lived with the ugly brown cabinets and Formica countertop. But you could not live with that kitchen. I could not live without round baby cats.

The round baby cats have taken to sleeping with the German shepherd  tiny tiny and big  blue mustard sahara  a June garden of columbine  red purple burgundy pink clematis  deep red and neon pink roses  and now the ice cream cone peonies of pale pale yellow and pink  lots of pink

You have just told me that Max cat is deformed. Eight toes is not deformed, eight is just enough. I have always wanted a very large cat with many toes and long hair. I have always loved what is odd. Maybe that is why I love you. You write of flowers and lushness and I think: how different this would have been if we had written this in the winter. This winter was so deep and white and silent, inside and out. I love the changes and the faith that comes with them.

In this collection we wanted to see what would happen given the co-existence in a short piece of two voices—not two voices from the same author—but voices from two distinct authors with some deep relation to each other  I have always been fascinated by the closely examined object by what happens when the writer turns her sight onto a specific object  in this case a lover  a loved person  an animal

We didn't, however, want to privilege couples—after all, we've all been single at some point, and some probably want to stay that way forever. So for those who have loved but don't have a partner or a lover who wanted to collaborate, we received poems, stories, musings. So we offer here some co-voiced objects experimental and not, a few solo ventures, some poems of love, not-love that we love. Our hope is that readers will delight in these, find a collaged portrait of what lesbian love is and might be.

---

Linda Smukler and Susan Fox Rogers met in Chicago on June 2, 1995, riding the subway on the way to the Lambda Literary Awards. They both had books nominated for the award, but neither of them won. An award, that is.

# morning

MUSIC BY PATRICIA MULLAN
WORDS BY LUCY JANE BLEDSOE

I awake at seven.

The cat is asleep between us, the sheets pulled neatly up to her black-and-white ruff. She accomplishes this by diving headfirst under the covers, then turning around and working her way back out until the covers reach the exact right spot.

She, the girlfriend, sleeps with a smile. *Zzzzzzz.*

I rise.

The cat considers her next move: more sleep, or breakfast? Choosing breakfast, she too rises, oh so slowly, stretching each hind leg just so, then walking to the edge of the bed, where she waits for me to lift her to the floor. Two years ago, we were told the cat had a couple of months to live. It was then we began allowing her into the bed, under the covers, between us nightly. It is this arrangement, I am sure, more so even than the daily IV fluids, that keeps her alive month after month after month.

I kiss her—the girlfriend, not the cat. *Get up, honey.*

*Zzzzzzzz.*

*Get up, honey.*

I hear something like a tinkle, almost chimes but lighter, more ethereal.

I lift the cat, who can but won't walk the stairs, and descend. As I go, I again suggest, *Honey, get up.*

Pausing on the stairs, I listen.

She's awake.

In the kitchen I make hot chocolate for her—the girlfriend, not the cat—and espresso-strength black tea for me.

*Cutekins, get up.* Oh, the words I can use for my butch girlfriend when no one else is within earshot.

I slip into my office for a quick E-mail check. When I return she is in the bathroom. I ask how she slept.

I silently rejoice that this will be a good-mood morning. I mention my manuscript on the kitchen table and wonder if she'll have time to read it before work.

We kiss. She says,

As I step into the shower, she slips on head-phones and begins her stretches. The cat joins her.

She showers, emerges, and the morning ratchets up a gear.

She irons and tells me a long story about the crazies at work. It goes like this:

I crack up and tell her about the woman at my reading last night who raised her hand to say she thinks I look better in my publicity picture than in person. We double over laughing, scream some more about the absurdity of humanity, and my girlfriend says,

Then we look at the clock.

Time, lost time, knives the hearts out of our good moods. I snatch up the cat and hold her while my girlfriend puts in the IV. The cat bucks her head, continuously, trying to disengage the needle, as the nutrients drip into the back of her neck.

We are both late.

We finish with the cat. My girlfriend throws on an outfit and throws back her hot chocolate.

she asks.

Because she is late and I know she will be upset at any delay, I lie and answer that her shirt looks great with those pants, and the socks, too, are fine.

She grabs her trombone, and its heft in her arm brings a smile, a re-swelling of enthusiasm for the day. She reminds me,

I know she has band practice tonight and wish her a good one. I don't mention the forgotten manuscript lying on the kitchen table.

We kiss.

We kiss again.

She kisses the cat.

Then me again.

Now the emergency of being late is no longer an emergency but simply a fact and we relax. We kiss some more. She tells another story, a long one, as if it's Sunday and we're sitting on the patio with lattes. She actually puts down her trombone and, in her wild-eyed way, tells me,

We

kiss more.

I watch her go down the walk, thinking that it is precisely this ability to speak the same language, while simultaneously preserving entirely separate languages, that explains our mornings, this lively joke on us, we who were going to have a simple affair, our years together.

I try to imagine having a girlfriend whose every utterance is comprehensible to me, who does not surprise me daily with puzzles of expression, and I shudder at the sadness and boredom of neatly parallel paths. Direct communication is highly overrated.

She starts the engine of her truck, rolls down the window. As usual, she revs the engine too hard, pulls into the traffic like she's driving the Indy 500 and roars up the street. Trailing out her open window, I hear or see or simply receive

Patricia Mullan plays trombone in two jazz bands, produces concerts, and is in charge of the Berkeley Public Library's art and music department. She also writes about jazz for radio and print media. Lucy Jane Bledsoe is the author of *Sweat* and *Working Parts,* and the editor of *Heatwave: Women in Love and Lust.* She teaches creative writing to adult learners (literacy students). Simone the cat passed into her next life on October 1, 1996.

# angela + camille = love*

## ANGELA ROMAGNOLI AND
## CAMILLE ROY

An interview over dinner at Ruby's Pizza.

**C:** What about those names you have for different parts of my personality—

**A:** You mean like *Jessica Horn.*

**C:** Yeah. Do you think that's normal?

**A:** That name came from Little Richard. Do ya remember Arsenio Hall interviewing Little Richard? It was after he'd been born again, and Arsenio was needling him about that televangelist Jim Bakker screwing Jessica Hahn. Little Richard looked up very sly and said, "Are you asking me about Jessica *Horn?*" Did you know she was the church secretary?

**C:** Really.

---

*Angela and Camille have been together for eighteen years, since Angela was a twenty-something and Camille was "chicken."

**A:** What a sexpot-looking 'ho she was.

**C:** That's your fantasy. That's why you call me by that name.

**A:** Nah. I know what you are. I wouldn't love you if you weren't weird, and you wouldn't love me if I weren't a smart-ass.

**C:** I guess.

**A:** When I first met you, I thought your middle name really was McCormick. Little did I know it was just an affectation.

**C:** What about Nadja?

**A:** That suited you better. . . . Listen, the fact that you were a femme for a while, that was just icing. You played it, it was a party, you were pretty good at it. But when I first saw you that winter in Michigan, wearing a huge Russian fur hat with earflaps, I knew what I was getting. A creature. It wasn't exactly what I wanted. I thought you might be more of a jock.

**C:** We have this odd chemistry. You're very socialized.

**A:** I try to teach you manners. My mother said, "If you can't say something nice, don't say anything." Didn't your mother teach you manners?

**C:** Of course not.

**A:** You're not allowed to give my femme friends who come over to the house the evil eye. What makes you think you can act that way?

**C:**   Whatever about manners. You're the only person I've ever known who used their good throwing arm to break bank windows. You were so rebellious.

**A:**   *Was?* I still am. I'm defiant every day. That's how I can go out in the world and be a butch. I hate to be in the closet, ever.

This is what was cute about you. On our second date, you brought your toothbrush. We ended up at my house, and you brushed your teeth. When I came out of the bathroom, there you were sitting on the bed, waiting for me. You'd taken all your clothes off. We had never even kissed.

**C:**   You seemed rough and sweet. Sexy to me.

**A:**   I felt tender after that.

**C:**   You are a hunk of tender. Sometimes I ask you why after all these years you still like me, and you say, "Well, I have to love somebody." That's true about you.

**A:**   It's your smell. I liked it from the first sniff.

**C:**   I wasn't comfortable with you for at least five years. I didn't know what to say.

**A:**   That's irrelevant.

**C:**   Why?

**A:**   At the start you were more fascinated by me than I was by you. It was my mouth. My bad-girl self. I had just gotten busted, and you were newly out, hanging with the dykes and drag queens and whores. It was all exciting to you. But that wasn't what was really going on. We didn't know what our process was going to be. How we would challenge each other. . . . You kept giving me things I wasn't expecting—in terms of the family stuff, the incest. As long as I fucked you regularly! Your horniness is irresistible, though I know I can't totally take it personally. Even though you were scared at first of my pussy.

**C:** I got over that ages ago!

**A:** Yeah.

**C:** What else should we talk about?

**A:** Did I tell you I talked to the salesman from Sprint?

**C:** No. So what?

**A:** We were talking about my account. Then he told me his stepfather was so racist he refused an operation because the hospital wouldn't promise him that the transfusion blood wouldn't come from somebody black. This Sprint guy had witnessed a lynching when he was a little kid, and his stepfather had a hand in. Anyhow, this guy was pretty shy. In high school he didn't date much, but there was this one girl he liked, she was his friend and really sweet. So he asked her to the prom, and they went. She was black. His stepfather disowned him after that. They didn't speak until he was dying. On his deathbed, the stepfather admitted he was wrong.

**C:** Jesus. The salesman told you that?

**A:** Yeah.

**C:** On the phone?

**A:** Yeah. I don't know why he told me all that.

**C:** I can't believe the things people tell you. Perfect strangers. What is that about?

**A:** Don't know. I told him I was a dyke, maybe that opened him up.

---

Angela Romagnoli wants it to be known that, thanks to her mixed Appalachian and Italian ancestry, she has been known as Hound Dog and Romeo Ravioli. She is a social worker and an ex-con (sort of). Camille Roy is a poet, fiction writer, and performer. Her most recent book is *The Rosy Medallions*.

## passing

MAUREEN SEATON
AND LORI MARSETTE

We were driving down the Kennedy having a great time guessing old groups Spinners Commodores La Belle maybe I was driving fast we'd been cold for a month not regular cold scary the kind that wears you down twenty forty below dark so cold you know hell is scratchy wool and miles of hard ice forget heat and everything suddenly stopped the Lincoln which was not our Lincoln but my sister's boyfriend's Lincoln not even his but the leased whim of a fired employee crashed into the back of a steel-gray Mercedes-Benz you could feel the ice eat your bones your bumpers the plastic grille curling up the back of the Mercedes Jesus that Lincoln imploded good old American the Mercedes owner said as we shook in the ridiculous cold cars whizzing down the frozen highway and Lori's arm shot across my chest like a mother's we'd been spoons sleeping on the sunny couch earlier while the temperature

14

reached a record low in Chicago my ex-husband used to say stop breathing on my back Maureen the only thing I remember about the crash is the way Lori's left arm reached out and saved me from ice crystals on the windshield she said whenever I breathe on her back she melts.

*I don't know what it is about women's pocketbooks. I still feel uneasy around them. I made up my mind a long time ago never to steal from women's purses. Especially since I knew that I was going to be around them quite a bit—okay, a lot. To steal seemed like defeating the purpose, blasphemy. I guess the butch in me respected that women's turf. There were women who told me, "Look in my bag and get so-and-so, etc., whatever." I never did. The other day Maureen, my wife, told me "Get money" from her purse; it was for our lunch. Even though it was money I had so proudly and finally been able to give to her, I still brought her her pocketbook, let her take out the money. Some rituals are sacred. Some subcultural mores must remain unchallenged. No matter how close I get to her, into her, it's still Maureen's purse/pocketbook/bag. The secret of its contents must stay secret. It's part of her seduction.*

When you lick me so light I can barely feel you—like that, the best jumping from the edge when the jump is violin, shards tinkling to the canyon floor, drops of light, I'm over my head in sixteenth notes, fragile as a river, that crystal.

Life is not all sex. But after seven years I'm amazed how your tongue reminds me of a puppy sweet woman yang and I love us in this swampy cow town where my father said years ago: "You like beef? This is the place!" Honey, you bring me back to lobster and butter clarified and running down the chin, that salty best part open open open when you suck it just right. I took a shower this morning, Friday.

*All last night I placed my hands on my pussy, moist still with the thought of you fucking me. I placed my hand on my pussy and brought my fingers up to my nose and I smelled you and I and strawberries. I wasn't sad. This morning I didn't want to shower but I had to. The world just doesn't understand a man/woman, woman/man smelling like a woman's woman loved by a woman. They don't trust it. Maybe because it's not that awful smell you get when semen is mixed in like whole worlds have died, whole spirits broken. I showered and cried and tried to console myself with the fact/promise that we will see each other again. Then I can give you my pussy once more and you can coax, then push yourself into that tiny opening that teases us. I can climb the walls and thrust my ass out to you. Make my pussy pout and tease and gape and devour your strawberry-gloved hand. Strawberry fields forever.*

Now the waitress at Baker's Square glides toward us like a boat, like a big mother, a head nurse, and writes down "pie." When she calls you "Sir," we know we've got it made. We feel high after the wisecracks on Clark, the narrowed eyes of young men on Estes, their threats to our anatomy, two women with the nerve to come biracial. "Take my hand," you say, reveling so hard in our sudden status as semilegitimate Americans you want to exploit every precious convention. We analyze you: slicked-back, pony-tailed hair, two earrings, soft red shirt. Must be the shoes, the tie, the way your eyebrow slides up as I slide my ass into the booth, the way you defer to me as if I were royalty. "You look like a woman to me," I whisper, so innocent the ice cream on my apple pie melts, so silky your biceps twitch beneath your shirt. "Kiss me," you say. And I do. Leaning across coffee like any ordinary female, sanctioned and smug to my toes with public approval, the tip of my tongue a sweet se-cret between us.

---

Maureen Seaton's latest book is *Furious Cooking*. Lori Marsette is a sculptor. They live in Chicago.

# love enough

 EILEEN MYLES

I looked into your big brown eyes the other
morning and I realized we've been together for
almost six years, and you're simply it, I love you,
and I give your long hairy body a stroke. I remember the day we met. I was walking down my
street and you were lying there on the sidewalk
with your brothers and sisters, sucking on your
mother's breasts. I got excited by this scene of
natural beauty and then you looked up. You
knew me! I felt that knowledge, we shared it and
we've been co-vivants ever since. Well there was
the exchange of fifty dollars, kind of our agree-
ment. For that you left your family and came
with me. The first summer I'd waltz you in the
kitchen. There was a song we both liked—King
Pleasure's "I'm in the Mood for Love." Just before we'd crack the bed, before I'd floss we'd do it
in the kitchen. Under that sweet note of light,
1990 when everyone was leaving town, had had

enough, we were plugging in quietly to something powerful. I remember the first time you saw grass. You almost broke my nose. I was lying on my back, in it, a small patch of it wrapped in hurricane link fence towered over by the large ugly public housing with balconies and great parking on First Avenue. I was comfortable with grass because I had lived on the earth for forty years, had known its pleasures seemingly forever, but you were new in it, were galloping in a rage of pleasure, hardly separating me from it so you stormed right up onto my face but you weighed less than twenty pounds then so you merely hurt me with your glee, but did not mangle. How you loved the shore! Cherry Grove, those small formal wavelets were monsters to you. It was almost cruel shoving nature at you and watching your unchained perceptions taking off.

Once I took off for a weekend that same first summer—as if I had my freedom anymore. I left you in a friend's care and when I returned my home was smeared with little ropes of turd all over the floor. The friend didn't understand that you didn't know how to be alone. Am I a lesbian mother? No I think I am your lover. You were part of the deal after that. I haven't done the best job, leaving you with wild boys for your second summer and your nipples looked scarred and I still hope it was some psoriasis rather than the ritual sex that I suspected. You are the jealous sort. I had a guest for a while and the first night you ran round the bed that held both my and her hairless bodies, barking and barking in a horror of displacement. As long as the guest lay in the bed, you were to find some other amenable piece of furniture. It was odd, you thought she was the boss for a while because she never laid with you. It's all sorted out now. A cool breeze surrounds the black-and-white female and the kind of tanned pinky one. I don't feel shy about your qualities. Let me describe them. White feet: four. Black tail with occasional white splashes. Black back, pink belly with sweet pale pink nipples. The lower belly a brighter pink, and still rather hairless from the surgery which I shall mention later. The head: a crest of whiteness pouring over the small part in your skull. I love your vulnerability. I place my fingers on your forehead, softly kneading the river of perhaps cartilage that must enable the wonderful range of expressions with which you greet the world, your living dog mask. Before we get to the honest eyes let me mention the twin shrub of peanut-butter-tan brow, little bumps of love and freedom that serve as echo chambers for the visuality of your eyes. Those. Always red, always sad, swimming through the sadness of what Rilke calls a dog's knowledge of death, but I say no. What she sees is a tunnel that recognizes no distinction between the initial blast of vivacity and the ultimate sinking into a world of grainy still things, the silly dream gone. She is in partnership with the utmost of veiny branches of time. What looks like sadness is a simple melancholy of knowing—it's all we've got and we're such fools in our clawing attempts at fixity, preservation, grandiose pit stops. She is wet with breath and people croon what a sad-looking puppy. And then they flash a peek at me and say we look alike. I shuffle my feet. I learned some.

Under her jaw is dirty white velvet. I don't keep my dog very clean. She smells like corn. Each foot bears three strong pads, balls of dog, rubbery marbles that lift her ever so slightly off the rug or the bumpy cement. One year or two her pads grew raw, chafed, bled, and I felt helpless. I know love. When she turned one I was forty-one. Three in 1993, six in '96, and I pray she lives till the year 2000, when she'll be ten and I turn fifty. I see an orange sun bobbing on the horizon and we move slow to that special land that ever retreats just beyond our melancholic visions. Once I dreamed she would be my immortality, or some continuation, but I watched her suffer intercourse twice and no "off-spring" came forth. The vet said some dogs don't want puppies. I didn't. But I got you and I think we're okay watching the line. I mean the line of the sea or the day or the window. The falling darkness and even keeping watch over the small sounds in the night that seem to talk about us in our wraggled bed. Our limbs tossed, our mothers gone, our lives complete. I eat my cereal, you're grunting in your bowl. It's what I've wanted all my life—a female all my own. Yet I know I will betray you.

---

Eileen Myles's newest book is *Maxfield Parrish: Early & New Poems* (Black Sparrow, 1995). With Liz Kotz she coedited the hit anthology *The New Fuck You: Adventures in Lesbian Reading,* from Semiotext(e), which won a 1995 Lambda Literary Award. Currently Myles is working on *Cool for You,* a trilogy of novels that comprise a female human history. Look for it in your bookstore soon. Rosie's currently asleep on the couch.

# portrait of carol and janelle

CAROL QUEEN AND
JANELLE DAVIS

Carol:

I identified as a lesbian for over a decade. Having relationships with women then was . . . well, not easy, exactly, but easier than it proved to be after I came out yet again, as a bisexual woman. Almost unconsciously, I stopped looking to dykes as love interests. At the same time I met an outrageous, loving bisexual man; how was I ever going to find a girlfriend now? (Except him, of course; he's a big old girlfriend.)

Unlike bisexual and bi-curious women who have never been immersed in dyke politics, I knew how unlikely it was that I'd find a lesbian lover who'd be tolerant, much less supportive, of my connection with Robert. I guess I stopped looking—only playing with women casually.

It's when you stop looking, you know, that you find.

Janelle:

**Words:** Carol's writing interested me first, before I ever knew her. I was a fan of the column she wrote for our local sex newspaper, and I read it for months before I knew what she looked like.

Carol:

In the meantime I was writing, publishing, getting a little notorious around town. When I was out and about and met a cute girl, it'd turn out I'd spoken to her Women's Studies class about porno when she was in college. I decided this might turn out to be an advantage.

Janelle:

**Sight:** The first time I saw Carol she was not entirely herself. A photo of her alter ego ran beside Carol's column that month; there she stood, wearing black lace lingerie and a blond wig. I already knew that she was brilliant, funny, well-informed, and deeply committed to preserving the liberties of sexual outcasts. Now I knew she was sexy too.

Carol:

She says she started out as my fan. I think that's a basic quality in a lover, actually. After all, I'm *her* fan, too.

Janelle:
**Sound:** I shouldered through the crowd and got as close to the stage as possible. I didn't want to miss a word of Carol's sex story or the chance to witness her reading it. Carol reads as well as she writes and her presence onstage is radiant, hot. My crush was born.

Carol:
Janelle and I were thrown together more than once over a couple of years' time, working together in various contexts. I thought she was an over-the-top, smart, funny, adorable babe, but I didn't cruise her—I knew she hung around with a boy.

Duh! So did I! What is *with* that?

Janelle:
**Sex:** Carol was giving a demonstration to a group of women about female ejaculation. Standing beside these women, I watched Carol fuck her G-spot with a metal dildo and eventually squirt for us. When I left the demo my jeans were soaked.

I had to find the courage to ask her out.

Carol:
We had one of those funny "I thought you'd

never ask" moments when we talked about going out. "What, you mean you had a crush on *me* all along? But I had a crush on *you!*"

You can never predict what kind of sparks will fly when you give a crush a good long time to get you juiced up, and then you finally have her skin against yours. Miss Sophisticated Porno Sex Educator (that's me) was left wide-eyed by how hot she was, how wild it felt, and oh, her pretty, pretty sounds. I can come just hearing her sounds.

Janelle:

**And?:** Yes, I asked her out. We started seeing each other and even teaching classes together. Once I was her fistee in a how-to class on vaginal fisting. After explaining the techniques in her fiercely articulate and charming way, our eyes locked and she slid her fist into my cunt, effortlessly. That's when I fell in love with her.

Carol:

I fell in love with *her* when she kept coming back for more, and that's exactly what I wanted . . . more.

Did I mention that Robert's presence with us is neither drama nor trauma?

I'd tried triangles with two women, and making it work was *hard.* But politics can't explain chemistry. And no matter what your Kinsey rating or plumbing, it takes special skills to create what we three have.

And what I have with Janelle is a loving, passionate friendship that's burned deep into my heart, but that won't allow for possessiveness. (That is, when it comes up, we talk about it until it goes away.)

Janelle is *mine* to about the same degree as my cat is.

She's my sweet, sassy love, because there is no one else occupying the place in my heart carved out for her. She's my kittycat, my pretty little sister, hot wet woman. I love her as she prowls, exploring the world.

---

Carol Queen was interviewed as a baby dyke for Ruth Baetz's book *Lesbian Crossroads.* Now she's an erotic writer, bisexual activist, and advocate for marginalized sexualities. When not doing workshops about the finer points of radical sexuality or talking to the media with Carol and Robert, Janelle Davis works at Good Vibrations.

## mazie's woman

NISA DONNELLY

You asked me how I come to be here, but you want a better answer than rain. Like rain ain't enough. How it seeps into the seams along the windshield. *Slap-patter. Slap-patter.* How you couldn't run the windshield wipers because the blades was worn through and there wasn't no way to get new. It was the war, you understand. Rubber was scarce. The rain come crawlin' up that glass, hit me in the face, like tears. As if I could remember how to cry. As if I ever knew how. Hell, I never even cried when that hook come loose, when that hunk of steel come at me and crushed my leg.

I was a long time waking up after that, years I guess, and then one day I come to and I was driving a 1939 Packard roadster convertible. Blue. With a Hartscloth top. I wasn't more'n twenty years old.

—And I was seventeen.
—On my way to Shreveport.
—And a virgin.
—I pulled off the highway because of the rain.

Every so often, I'd send her a postcard, made
out that things were going better. One had a picture of a pink hotel in Miami Beach. She's still
got it, stuck up over the bed. Hell, I didn't have
the heart to tell her that I found a couple dozen
of them in the trash, stuck together. Sent one to
ever'body I could think of. She was the only one
thought it was special, though. Called her twice,
from a pay phone in a diner across from where I
was working. I liked that she missed me. Maybe
that's why I came back, just to see if anything had
changed. And it had some. She was putting up
motel cabins back of the gas station. Figured with
the war ending there'd be call for tourist cabins
along the river. That is how I knew she was smart.
And I was smart enough to stay when she asked.

—I never asked.
—I could hear you calling. Wherever I was, I
     could hear you.
—But I never asked.
—But I answered.

Miami Beach. Sarasota. Atlanta. After a while I gave up paying attention to the cities and just tried to remember the names of the states. Those were bad times. I spent some months on the oil rigs down in Texas. Back to the boats in Louisiana. Then over to Florida. Picked up a few days' work here and there. It was always the same: "We can't use you full time, but I've got this engine that nobody can figure out. You put that right, I'll make it worth your while." Worth my while was always half what they would've paid a white man. But I did it. And they paid me. Or wished they had. The rest is probably still wishing they had. I have ways of getting my point across.

Two years was gone since I'd seen her. Seen that truly remarkable sight when she was showing me the path down to the river. The wind caught her dress, blew the skirt up, and there before me was the roundest, pinkest, and I don't mind saying prettiest ass I'd ever hoped to see. Bare naked. By the time she'd pushed her skirt down, I knew I was in love. She'll swear to this day that she didn't have her underpants on because it was hot, but the truth is she never did wear them. From the outside, she was all priss and polish, and underneath she didn't wear panties.

I'd been thinking about that pink round slice of heaven, when I saw a sign—Tourist Cabins, Fried Catfish, Cold Beer—with an arrow pointing toward a blacktop that didn't seem to lead anywhere except down to the river. And I ain't nobody's idea of a Christian, but I said, "Thank you, God." I don't mind saying that I was lost. I kept a little card that told how to find her in my wallet. But it all went one night outside Rockridge, Tennessee, when I fell in with some shiny drunks and the local sheriff pulled us in. Got the wallet back. Empty. But I figured that if I followed the river, I'd sooner or later hit on the right blacktop.

—You forgot there were two sides to the river.
—I know it, I'm getting to that part.

Eighty-seven signs and blacktops. Some of them looked familiar. But each time, the closer I got to the river, I knew something wasn't right. At the road's end there was sometimes pretty good catfish and always cold beer, but it was never the right road. I'd ask about the landing. Some said they'd heard of it, but a long time ago, thought it got washed away in the last flood, or the one before that. Others just shook their heads, like flies was buzzing through. Finally, I

31

found a place where there was an old man. "You're on the wrong side of the river, son." Not many mistook me for a man, but he did and I was grateful.

Nothing along that road looked more or less familiar than any of the other blacktops I'd been on. Scrappy fields, a couple of farmhouses, then a raggedy, hanging-on river town. To this day, I don't know if she was surprised to see me. She came walking out into the parking lot, dressed in a white summer dress with big red strawberries printed all over it. Smiling. Pushing back her hair, which had gone all wet and curly from the rain. She was wearing red high-heeled sandals. No stockings. The strawberries wilted against her legs.

—You waited for me to come to you.
—And so you did.
—You were crying.
—No, it was just the rain. I remember.

Nisa Donnelly is the author of *The Love Songs of Phoenix Bay* and *The Bar Stories: A Novel After All*. Her short fiction and essays are found in several anthologies, among them *Women on Women* volumes 2 and 3, *Sister and Brother*, *Queer View Mirror*, *Heatwave*, and *Erotic Interludes*. A renegade writer raised in the backwaters of America, she lives and writes in San Francisco.

# where there be dragons

MARGARET ERHART AND ANN BAKER

Here we are. We live on this crooked finger of land, this geographical beckon where everybody else just visits. We have ocean on one side, bay on the other, ponds in between. Some itinerant dunes temporarily pinned by pines and dressed in smart travelers' fashion: *Uva ursi,* beach grass, poison ivy, *Rosa rugosa*—clothes you'd never leave home without. Our house in a hollow between two big amblers. To the south the marsh; north, the county road. We don't own much furniture—have things on loan and make stuff from other stuff that's drifted onto the bay beach. Just the other day we carried home a ladder, a good one with a broken rung. What's a wooden ladder doing out at sea? No gutters to clean but the trough of the waves filled up with foam.

The first time Ann and I went walking on that beach we had so much to say it was hard to speak. I noticed Ann's sturdy walk, how she hopped barefoot from rock to rock in her long tangling raincoat, how every other rock seemed to interest her and find its way into her pocket, as well as pieces of colored nylon line. It was a collecting expedition that day. We collected the small gestures and physical facts of each other that we liked and we decided without deciding to go on and collect more. I collected her feet. Useful, squarish feet with long toes that could pick up pebbles and shells. Hands similar, fingers long and tapered. Tapered fingers were something I'd only read about. They were like candles, darker than beeswax. I imagined the scent of them, the scent of honey and salt. On flat ground she walked as if she were climbing stairs, a lift at the end of each step that hinted at a kid who'd traveled on tiptoe and was trained down.

I never go onto that beach without thinking of that day when we said almost nothing to each other and all the other days when we said less. We said more on the bay side than on the ocean. The ocean beach was a serious place for us, exhilarating and tragic and burning with the cold salt of the Atlantic as it abraded our home shore. The bay beach was slower and calmer, the place where we first discovered our connection and were briefly not frightened by the power of it. We could laugh there. We were friends there. When it turned we went to the ocean for its vast anonymity, for the erasure of its tides. To look back and see no print of our bodies was both necessary and impossible. I felt broken by every breaking wave of the ocean. The bay with its human trash at high-water mark was a world where what people lost came back to them, with edges eroded, colors faded, essences tempered but more revealed. Whatever we threw away or lost or forgot came back. I think of the bay as a body of mercy.

—M. E.

I spent yesterday at the beach where Margie and I first touched. It is what we in Truro call the back shore, the great bend from the elbow of the Cape to its fingertips that blocks the North Atlantic the way a person puts her arm up to ward off a blow. It is a dramatic place of steep, sheared-off dunes and long rolling breakers. At low tide lean, clean sandbars break the ocean into pale green pools and shadowy blue depths. It is vastly impersonal, dangerous, uninterested in puny human events.

For years this beach was my refuge. The wavering line of pebbles at the tideline was a seam in a great cloth, and I followed it. My mother used to say, "You're not the only pebble on the beach, you know." At Longnook I was content to be one among millions, present in a place where the distinctions between animate and inanimate, individual and multiple were unimportant.

That wasn't true the spring Margie and I first felt our pull toward each other. Then the beach was the edge of our exquisite anxiety. The magnificence of the place was just backdrop. There was a painful joy in me that I could feel traveling down each long nerve, could feel branch and burn along every surface of myself. I felt hollow, my own blood pounding like storm surf. I was afraid and fearless. Too small against the elements and greater than any fury or glory they could muster. At night, when we walked, the waves rumbled toward us. It was as though we had come into the Grand Central Station of the universe, all black marble with the ceiling lights high above us hazy as the ocean fog drifted in around us. Without sight the other senses probed the darkness, searching for what had not yet taken form. We were luminous in those soft black nights but we suffered. Both on a platform from which either might catch the train away from this new joining, back into the familiar countries of our previous lives.

Years ago I stood on the Longnook dunes in a winter storm and watched a small bird blow right past me like a dry leaf. That late spring the wind blew and we tried to hold our ground. We tucked in against the dune and sheltered each other as well as we could. Nothing broke the flatness of the Atlantic out to where it met the wall of sky. It was easy to imagine that they didn't meet, that the water poured endlessly down into darkness. I understood the old mapmakers' instinct to letter "Beyond this be dragons" around the margins of what they knew. I, too, feared the dragons. But we dared them together. We still do. They sleep or stalk other prey for stretches of time but sometimes they still come very near. They are so primal, quick to strike, always knowing our weaknesses. But we are getting to know them, too. Our eyes are getting sharper. We know where to step. We warn each other. "Beyond this be dragons." And then we take each other's hand.

—A. B.

---

M.E.: We are rushing to catch a plane, so I am thinking for two. Ann and I met in a writing class I was teaching. She unnerved me, kept teaching me. Which is teaching at its best. We both had other lives hurtling to completion. "Resist, resist" was (briefly) my motto. We risked a lot to be together—it works. We live in a two-hundred-year-old house in Truro, Massachusetts. Ann's a psychologist. Me, I'm a novelist. At least by day.

## struck

### JOAN LARKIN

You got me scared right off the bat
with your saying you'd like me to buy this
     house
& you'd had a hot love affair with a strong
     woman—
a quick confession. You're as reckless as I am.
You say you love me, you're happy I'm here.
     You say, Come
spend the summer; I may go to Minnesota
     though.
*On my own so fast!* I think, staring at the tad-
     poles—
there are thousands wriggling in this little lake
with everything in it, near it, above it, stirring
fin, wing, tail. I rub the dog, you rub my leg,
     we talk
& groom ourselves like seals against each other.
Your thoughts shock me like last night's light-
     ning

striking right by the house. The house rolls
& your cups in the kitchen's thunder peal as
        they fall.

Joan Larkin's collections of poetry include *Housework, A Long Sound* (in which this poem appears), and *Cold River*. She coedited the anthologies *Amazon Poetry, Lesbian Poetry,* and *Gay and Lesbian Poetry in Our Time*. She lives and writes in New York City and teaches in the Goddard College M.F.A. program in creative writing. She received a 1996–97 National Endowment for the Arts fellowship for poetry.

# falling in love from her coast to mine

AMBER HOLLIBAUGH AND
MARJ PLUMB

These letters were written between October 1992 and January 1993. Marj lived and worked in San Francisco at the time; Amber was working and living in New York City. This was the first series of letters between us as we tried to navigate our growing romance and the distances and obstacles between us.

*Amber—*

*Every time we've been together this week, I could have talked with you for twice as long (at least). You know, you have touched me deeply and in ways I can't even begin to express. I am a romantic and I do believe in magic. This week my sense of you was so full and powerful. At times I felt your presence as a friend, other times as a lover. There were actually times when you were talking that I felt the presence of a sister of mine. I never felt you as my mother—that is the very good*

40

*news! I am so very excited about this journey. I want to know how it feels to have deep intimacy with someone without sex. I want us to start learning about each other. I guess I'm the first writer, so I'll start . . .*

*Marj*

*Dear Marj,*
*Here's the end of what I thought, then I'll go back to the beginning. You're wonderful. And much which I felt and understood about who you are (not who you're afraid you are) was there in the letter. Umm. It's hard for me, this sorting through and sorting out of feelings and reasons for what I'm doing with you and with myself. I am hurting right now. Hurting to see you, hurting from the places that are still open scars from a long marriage and another recent breakup, hurting in a wordless place where my fears overshadow reason. Still, I am intrigued with my passionate feelings for you. I kinda don't know what happened. It's like a dust storm suddenly swirling up in the middle of an empty place. I see you fear that my only "real" desire for you is sexual. It is okay with me that we move forward the way you want, Marj, really. But for me, I guess I feel so vulnerable in actually showing the concrete geography of my desire to a woman I want to be touched by, that it seems risky in either place. This is the struggle for me in the passion of wanting your hands moving my*

*body forward and it is also the fear of being a compan-*
*ion to your spirit during the daylight. I see the power of*
*you, your nerve. I am deeply attracted to power and to*
*a woman who can take me under. . . . Dammit. It's*
*5:30 in the morning and I can't get you out of my*
*mind or out of my body. I am telling you stories that*
*I'm afraid to reveal and still you don't go away from*
*me. Then I am on my knees reaching up to kiss you, my*
*hands are in your hair, you are unbuttoning my blouse*
*and pulling me to your mouth, I am gone.*

*Amber*

*Dearest Amber,*
*I was awed by the power of your words. I can't remem-*
*ber a time when I have read something that was writ-*
*ten so powerfully. My dear, you amaze me. I could*
*easily begin relying on you to encourage me, to tell me*
*how wonderful and smart I am, and I might even*
*begin believing you. But I can't take on that type of re-*
*liance anymore. I need to know that when I am sixty*
*and alone I will know how to decorate an apartment,*
*how to cook for one, and what I'll say to the voices at*
*three A.M. . . . This space between friends and lovers is*
*no-woman's-land. As slowly as we move through this*
*space, feelings, ideas, thoughts, and fears move around*
*us very quickly, urging, coaxing, pleading for us to*
*move more rapidly. I hope you don't go away.*

*Marj*

*Hello Darlin',*
*I can't get over the presence you have in my mind and in my days. Without warning, you have swept inside me and I hear you from the inside out . . . stunning me with your laughter and your insight, pleasing me with your intelligence. I can feel you near me, in me, with me, like few people I have carried in my heart. All day, I've been talking to you in my head, telling you stories, hearing your laughter, watching your face as it reflects all the feelings you try to keep back. I think you are astonishing. A stupendous gift in my life.*

Amber

*Amber—*
*I think back to when we met in L.A. I can't believe I am now falling in love with the woman who sat across from me at dinner. The woman who completely invaded my heart and mind. The woman who I dreamed about for months later. I met you for a nanosecond in time but I could still recall your power, sexuality, vitality, energy, and passion. I could still feel your leg touching mine.*

Marj

*Hi Baby,*
*I'm scared, Marj. Scared of showing myself without the sex to get me over—it's like you know that people want you because you can do things? Well, people want*

*me because I can manifest heat and submission and passion. But when I really want someone on my own terms, there's also the part that's fearful and angry and needy . . . not hot. Anyway, it's fine that we be close, be friends at first, though I insist on the pleasure of trying to seduce you; you can't deny a high femme challenges.*

*Amber*

---

Amber Hollibaugh and Marj Plumb are in a long-term primary butch-femme relationship with lots of heat and lots of struggle. Amber Hollibaugh is director of the Lesbian AIDS Project at Gay Men's Health Crisis and a filmmaker, writer, and community organizer. Marj Plumb is director of the Office of Lesbian and Gay Health for the New York City Department of Health. She is also a writer, speaker, and community organizer.

# duet for two buns
## and a patty

MARIANNE DRESSER AND
ZÉLIE POLLON

*Marianne and Zélie are in M's studio apartment, sitting on the couch. It's early evening, after work, and they are hungry. Z speaks:*

What should we do for dinner?

I dunno. I want meat. I crave a big juicy hamburger.

I could eat a hamburger.

Let's go to Hot 'n' Hunky.

Or we could go to Sparky's. It's closer. Or we could just get takeout and come back here, or go to your house if you want.

Look, why don't we go to Safeway and get some ground beef. I have some corn pasta at home I could heat up.

I don't want sticky leftover corn pasta, I want a hamburger.

I'll make you a nice fresh hamburger patty. . . .

*As they put on their jackets and head downstairs to*

*the street, M contemplates Z's offer. She's not quite convinced.*

On a bun? I want a hamburger on a bun with cheddar cheese and pickles and tomatoes and red onion—the works. Do you have all that stuff?

Yeah, yeah.

And no spelt—I want buns. We'll get a whole pack and put the rest in the freezer. I have to have real buns. Do you have red onion and tomatoes?

Yes, I just said so!

*The two walk down Church Street toward Market.*

When was the last time you checked?

(*sternly*) Marianne . . .

It's just that your vegetables very often tend to be somewhat venerable by the time you get around to them.

Marianne, I just bought a goddamn red onion at the market not twenty minutes ago!

This is getting to be too much trouble. Let's just go get takeout. But not Sparky's. If we're gonna do fast food, it has to be *good* fast food. Let's go to Hot 'n' Hunky.

Whatever. Why don't you call ahead and we'll go and pick it up and go straight to my house.

Calling takes too much time. Can we just go?

*They arrive at Z's Toyota in the Safeway parking lot, and get in. The engine turns over, but won't start.*

*This happens a lot. Z mournfully rests her head on the steering wheel.*

Okay, look. I'll go call and order the food. By the time I get back the car will start. What do you want?

*Z waves her hand dejectedly. M gets out of the car and walks to a nearby phone booth. Z continues trying the engine. After a few minutes the car starts. She drives toward M, who gets into the car, fuming.*

Zélie, I swear . . . I dial 411 and no one answers, so I dial the operator and ask her to put me through to Information. So she puts me through to 411, it rings about a thousand fucking times and no one answers. *No one answers!*

*Z drives the four blocks to Hot 'n' Hunky. The place is packed, the line spilling out onto the sidewalk.*

I told you we should've ordered ahead. Let's go to Sliders.

Zélie, I *tried* to phone ahead, remember?

*They drive around the corner and find a parking place right in front of the burger joint on Castro Street, which seems auspicious.*

I'll stay here and keep the car running. Get me one, too.

Don't you want to come in with me? The car will start.

(*sighing*) I guess we might as well stay here and eat.

*They walk into Sliders and order at the counter.*

Will you buy my burger?

You want *me* to buy your burger?

Sure. Why not? It won't kill you. You always say you'll take me out and you never do. You owe me.

*M pays. They wait. And wait. House music blares. They nuzzle by the condiment bar. Noticing the wilted lettuce, days-old tomatoes, and crusty mayonnaise, they decide to change their order to takeout. After waiting another five minutes, they are finally given two unappealing dried-up burgers in styrofoam containers. Exchanging "uh-oh" expressions, they gamely file back to the condiment bar and pile on lubricants, then return to the car. As she gets into the car, Z drops a plastic knife smeared with mustard on her pants.*

Where in hell did that knife come from?

I put it there. I thought you might need it. Shit.

*Z turns the key. Nothing.*

Great, *ju-u-st* great. . . .

*The odor of grease begins to fill the car's interior.*

I can't believe you chose *this* over my offer of a fresh homemade burger.

*I* said Hot 'n' Hunky. This place was *your* idea. . . . (*silence*) My fries are cold and they don't have any salt on them. Want some?

48

No. I'm grossed out enough by my own food, thanks. God, the smell of rancid oil is fierce.

*Z tries the engine again. Nothing. They eat in silence. Stylish gay couples pass on the sidewalk and a disco thump emanates from the uniform bar. They look over at each other, each hunched over her Styrofoam container, and burst out laughing.*

You know, if I have to sit in a broken-down car eating some disgusting hamburger, there's no one else I'd rather be with.

Me too, babe.

---

Marianne Dresser and Zélie Pollon live, work, play, and occasionally squabble in San Francisco. When not writing and editing, they enjoy traveling and scuba diving. They believe spirited debate enlivens any relationship.

# dream

BY GERRY GOMEZ PEARLBERG

*For A.*

I dreamed I had a fireplace
and that you slept beside me there.
I watched us as if from another body,
and longed to be me, warm in the blaze of
    resting
against you.

I dreamed of what wakefulness excluded,
of dust motes in air, those tiny hope motels
made incandescent by negligee light.

I dreamed the light was alive.

I dreamed you drank oat tea in the 4 A.M. dark,
the white cup traveling from lips
to lap like a satellite.
I read you poetry and kissed you above

a copper book's soft cover,
over and over.

I dreamed of the raven's first call
from its branch outside my window,
so close, and of those black feathers ruffling
under insinuations of wind.

I dreamed of the first light's hesitant grain
moistly suckling the windowpane behind the
　　　white shade.

I dreamed we talked of honey and lions,
of home-grown watercress,
ex-lovers and their exes.

I dreamed you said, "You make it hard
not to love you."

After that I couldn't sleep.

Gerry Gomez Pearlberg's poetry and prose have appeared in
*Women on Women 3, modern words, Plazm, Chelsea,* and
*The Beloit Poetry Journal.* She is the editor of two poetry an-
thologies: *The Key to Everything: Classic Lesbian Love Poems*
(St. Martin's Press, 1995), a 1995 Lambda Award nominee,
and *The Zenith of Desire: Contemporary Lesbian Poems About
Sex* (Crown, 1996).

My Over-40 Wish List: Attractive, available woman over 40 with a sense of humor and artistic sensibility. Serious but not heavy-hearted. I am a literary-minded, seasoned lesbian who's been around the relationship block a few times but would like to try again.

*Hi MEB,*
*I fit the description, although I cannot claim to be a seasoned anything. I have been involved with men in two long-term relationships most of my life, but always there was a woman in the background. Two years ago she and I finally got together, but before any real relationship had a chance to develop, she was diagnosed with breast cancer and in her anger, turned away.*

*After that I decided I owed it to myself to understand what this woman had been doing in my life all those years. About six months later, I started going*

*with another woman, but she was not a wise choice,
and it soon ended in disaster.*

*I am a writer, teacher, and freelance editor. Sort of
the Blanche DuBois type. I would do well with a soft
butch, as I don't think it would do for both of us to be
nervous, fluttery butterflies.*

At the age of fifty, having answered the above
ad, I suddenly found myself dating again, and,
like many who have been out of circulation a
long time, I felt as inexperienced and gauche as
a teenager. Worse, actually, for I had never dated
a woman.

When Maureen and I first got together, I
imagined all kinds of strange rituals and codes of
dress and behavior would be required of me. I
had read enough ads to know that lesbians splin-
ter into countless subgroups. There were butches
and femmes, lipstick lesbians, dykes on bikes,
soft butches, lesbians who dated only Asian sisters, S/M lesbians, lesbians who wouldn't date
you unless you came in bulk.

I didn't think I wanted to be tied up or wear
leather (well, maybe for one night). If I fell in
love with a woman, would she want me to give
up wearing skirts and heels, lipstick and my
grandmother's long, dangly earrings? At this
stage of life, didn't I have the right to think my

permanent identity had been forged? On this point, however, I now see I was wrong.

Seven months and nine days have passed since Maureen and I met at the Paradise Muffin Co. on Eighth Avenue in Chelsea, ostensibly for coffee but really to check each other out. I got there first. Insides a mess. So nervous I was sure, when the kid behind the counter said, "Okay, lady, what'll you have?," that I would revert to my adolescent habit of vomiting before dates. Then, out of the corner of my eye, I saw a small, slim, self-contained-looking woman approach a table for two against the wall and seemingly in slow motion reach out to hook her umbrella over the back of the chair. Deliberate, cautious and quiet as a cat, I thought. Serious. *Oh dear, she will think I am so silly.* Long, angular face like mine. Red hair. *No one with red hair could ever not like me.*

I turned back to the kid and ordered my cappuccino. As he rushed off to get it—*Why is she taking so long?*—I checked her out sideways one more time. She took off her raincoat, hung it on the chair. When she turned around, my heart sank. There on her feet were sensible brown oxfords. Could I really fall in love with someone in lesbian shoes?

*How can I escape? Is there no back door? Oh my God, she's coming closer!*

"Martha?" I heard at my elbow.

The next seven months have gone by in a blink.

On occasion, she still puts on her lesbian shoes.

I never do.

Closely I watch this woman I've come to cherish as she flutters about the room, seeking space, locating a perch for herself. *Where did she come from?* I often ask myself. I posted my wish list on AOL and she appeared.

I had done a lot of healing from earlier brokenhearted. And it seemed as if I had fulfilled a requisite period of waiting. Feeling small in my queen-sized bed, though queenly. Missing her without knowing who she was. Dating without finding her until dating began to seem as if it were a distinctly stressful activity with little or no relationship to love.

We met for coffee at the Paradise Muffin Co., my choice, which I believe I made in hopes the name might foreshadow our union. I said I had red hair. She said she did, too. We found each other at first glance. I already knew her last name was my mother's maiden name. We could be far distant cousins. We had a certain likeness to each other. By the end of an hour, she felt familiar. On the street she said she'd enjoyed our meeting and left me with a command to call her. I went away light and relieved of the burden of not knowing who would call whom.

I thought that as the seasoned lesbian I would need to take charge of the seduction, but she met me at every juncture and turned a few corners herself. We wove together, moving through moments of fear like thread snagging, then working free. Love makes life want to work.

I was tired of relationships that were constituted of struggle, even proud struggle, or that took place in the therapist's office. I wanted something that was often easy. *This is.*

---

Maureen Brady is the author of *Give Me Your Good Ear, Folly,* and *The Question She Put to Herself,* as well as three books of nonfiction. M. E. Hughes is the author of *Precious in His Sight* and two books of nonfiction. They live in New York City, where they are book doctors and teachers of creative writing. Together they run a summer writing program in Woodstock, New York.

How they met:

The time is 1981, the place is rural Tennessee . . .

"So you lived in New York, huh?" says Merril. "Me too—in the sixties. So where'd you hang out?"

"Kookie's, of course," Mary replies. She never would dream of slumming in the downtown bars like the Sea Colony or the Washington Square. "Where'd *you* hang out?"

"Oh, the Sea Colony, mostly," Merril tells her. Mary looks away. Merril continues: "Sometimes I'd go to the Washington Square, too, and every once in a while my buddy and I would go to Kookie's and cruise the snobs." She chuckles. "We'd usually end up going home with one of them, too."

Mary's interest revives. This still might be

worth pursuing. "Oh. Yeah? So what were you—butch or femme?"

Merril draws herself up to her full eight feet eleven. "Need you ask?" she drawls. "And what were you?"

Mary crosses her legs coyly. "Oh, femme, femme, of course," she lies.

"I love you," Mary declares as the relationship gets under way, "and I want a future with you."

"I love you," Merril agrees. "And I don't want to live with a lover. I don't want to blend our families. I like my own space and my own separate life. I'm not very good at coupleness. And I want a future with you, too."

Mary: ??????????

Mary always had been monogamous. Merril always had not been monogamous. After six or seven years together, as one might expect, things came to a head, but not necessarily as one might have expected:

Mary was seeing another woman. "What does it matter," she says to Merril, "since you're not monogamous anyhow?"

"But I've become monogamous in our relationship," Merril replies, "because I love you and I know it's important to you."

"Well, I didn't really know that," Mary responds, "so I started seeing someone else; but I'm not being non-monogamous, I'm just going with the program."

Merril: *??????????*

Mary: After many years of struggle, I finally found a way to maintain our relationship at the level of intimacy we both needed. I left her. She didn't notice. After several months, I realized that I missed her a lot, so I re-entered the scene. She didn't notice that, either.

"I don't want to be part of your karmic agenda!" says Mary.

"Sorry," Merril replies, "but you *are* part of it, and I'm part of yours, so we may as well work it out."

They go into therapy together to help work it out, and Merril meets a woman through one of the therapists. The therapists encourage Mary and Merril to break up. Mary and Merril break up with the therapists, and still are together to this day, doing their karmic agendas, and working it out.

On their tenth anniversary together, Merril gives Mary a double-chambered crystal geode from her farm, and a card that reads: *To Mary—our ten years together/our relationship/our selves/our hearts/our lives: together, yet separate/separate, yet together/beautiful/complete/the perfect jewel.*

Mary looks forward to seeing what Merril will give her on their twentieth anniversary. Merril is working on it.

Now, fourteen years into their relationship, Mary must spend much of the time far away in Philadelphia to do her work. Merril remains in Tennessee. Their relationship remains the same.

On one of her visits home, Mary says to Merril, "I miss you."

"Well, as you know," Merril replies, "I don't really ever *miss* people, but," she hastens to reassure Mary, "if I *were* to miss anybody, it would be you."

---

Mary and Merril did this piece long distance over the telephone, each doing her share in her typical fashion and agreeing on the outcome. They both have developed very good self-preservation skills.

# the kim poems

ROXXIE

KIM POEM #1

I have a friend who is so sexy that wherever she goes, all the girls fall for her.

My friend has a partially shaved head. She's so sexy and butch that even my best gay-boyfriend wants to have sex with her.

The problem is that every girl I meet drops me the second she meets my sexy shaved-head friend.

Should I shave my head too?

Even if I had a head start on getting a date, my friend comes in at the most amazing clip. Sometimes she feels sorry for me and tells me what to say to girls, but even when she helps me, I can't keep up with her. I concede all races to her.

She gets every girl, so finally I invented an imaginary girlfriend named Kim.

Kim is a stewardess, okay? So she travels a lot. That's why you've never met her. She is always my date. She's in the bathroom a lot, or answering a page, or she had to go home early.

Kim, Kim, Kim.

## KIM POEM #2: KIM

I invented Kim to bother my ex-girlfriend. See, my ex-girlfriend is going out with someone, and she told me they are having, um, sex.

I had to get back at her. My mother always said, "All's fair in love and war."

## KIM POEM #3: SOMEONE

Someone agreed to lie for me and say she saw me and Kim together. Someone else agreed to say she saw us out to breakfast on a weekend morning in the Mission, and that she saw us holding hands. Someone else agreed to say, "Yes, Kim is very pretty," with a wistful tone in her voice. Someone else agreed to say that she wanted to have Kim in the biblical sense because Kim is so pretty.

Someone else agreed to say she was a redhead.

Someone else agreed to say that she was sure that "We WERE IN LOVE."


## KIM POEM #4: CLAIRE

I told my soccer team about Kim. I thought it would make them laugh. Besides, I like to share things with my teammates. We are, um, close.

I thought they would laugh because imaginary friends are supposed to disappear at age nine, and I am thirty-four.

I was right. They laughed.

But then Claire, who plays outside halfback and can run for days at a time, said that she was going out with Kim, too.

Claire said that Kim didn't actually take all those business trips she said she'd taken, but she'd been seeing her.

I got the feeling Claire thinks she is a better lover than me.

Claire said she has made love to Kim so many times that Claire said her name is the one etched deep into Kim's heart.

"Not so," I told Claire. "Mine."

## KIM POEM #5: A GIRL

I told a real girl the story about Kim, the whole story, especially the part about Claire. Something strange happened.

She offered to come to a soccer game and introduce herself to Claire and say that her name was Kim and that she was a stewardess.

Then something stranger happened. She took me home with her. *Great,* I thought. Then she had sex with me. I thought, *My lucky day, my lucky day.*

A few days later the real girl was supposed to come to my soccer game. I was waiting to play this joke on Claire. I waited and waited all game, but the real girl never showed up.

Maybe I should shave my head.

---

Valentine's Day, 1995. I send a woman I've been dating a dozen long-stem roses. She calls and blows me off. Later that day, I go to play soccer and forget all about love. I play soccer six times a week. My metabolism changes, I have to sleep more, and eat really healthy foods, and don't really have time for, um, you know. The Kim poems were born out of that ultra-athletic time.

Roxxie founded and edits *Girljock Magazine.*

# step by step

### KITTY TSUI AND ANDREA PEDIT

I sit here in my office, unable to concentrate on the work at hand. Many things need to be done, but my mind wanders off like a child who has spied something gleaming in the path ahead. I didn't want to leave you this morning, your smooth warm skin, so dark next to mine.

it was unexpected. the touch
of your hand, the instant
energy between us.

We are alike in many ways, you and me, and while I like that about us, I am drawn even more by our differences. You come from a place unknown to me; you speak a different language, come from a different country and culture, have chosen as your life's work a vocation I have never known. And the physical differences: your brown eyes, such a wonderful contrast to mine, your skin a rich hue unlike any other I have known.

i am wounded, vulnerable
and raw, yet strangely
not afraid.

I fear you, Kitty Tsui: the hurt you could cause me, the hard work that I think will be necessary for both of us . . . But with this risk comes the potential for great love, the likes of which I have never known.

why is it my heart can be
open and trusting
and unafraid?

We are being tested here. We both say we have learned many things unable at times to hide our disappointment at how long it took. But my past has been perfect for having led to the richness of emotion and feeling that I'm experiencing only now, with you . . . I know there are many things yet to learn, for that is the nature of living. I've always felt the definition of a fool was someone who failed to learn and grow from their experiences. I feel your grandmother and my mother would not have consorted with fools.

one step at a time i will walk
with you, towards you,
one step at a time.

It is for me one step at a time too, but I will tell
you I like this path a great deal. It is lit by the
sun and the moon both, and I will continue to
walk it for as long as I can.

the other night in bed
Andrea said:

you are a pretty woman,
and i love you.

the words touched
my heart. i opened, opened.

It is hard to put into words the feelings I am
deriving from your presence in my life. It
has been . . . pure, unadulterated pleasure, ex-
citement, laughter, raw sexual energy, sadness,
romance, the entire gamut. That broad range,
and the intensity of it, is what I love sharing
with you. I wanted you to know.

the words whispered in the dark
touched my heart.

Kitty Tsui and Andrea Pedit are both Virgos, born a year and a week apart. Between them they have a dog and three cats. Kitty is the author of *Breathless* and *Sparks Fly*. Andrea is not a writer. She waits patiently—well, sometimes—for Kitty's book tours to end.

## name calling

TRACY YOUNG

In my book, to love is to name. Not that I am the original author of that impulse: Humbert Humbert tongue-tapped down the hardcore consonants of his Lo-li-ta; and when Al Green sang "Call Me," he was talking about an invocation, not AT&T. But neither is love particularly original, except in the particulars. And what love and naming have in common is the will to possess, which may be why we name all sorts of possessions, to the extent of seeming, well, possessed— or at least guilty of lusting after things.

Cats, being predators, name themselves. Who they are is something they give off, a pheromone. For instance: Cole. The name sprang unbidden to mind the moment I clapped eyes on him, like love at first sight—which is pretty much what I felt: a sudden rapture both irrational (he was as homely as a rat) and inevitable. Cole was inevitably, and simply, Cole, until a few months later, when my lover and I were watching *Roots* on TV, at which point we began referring to Cole as "Kunte Cole," and the kitten I bought for my lover as Kizzie because she looked a bit like Leslie Uggams.

Or take Raisin, a shimmering black Burmese with a Mae West walk. She started out as Aretha, but was far too humble to bear the weight of a name like that, so she became known as Raisinette, then Raisin. And when an otherwise uninspired romantic partner started singing, "Look out, here she comes, she's a Bag Eater" because the cat had an appetite for plastic, Raisin became Bag. It was the high point of the affair. With the girl.

The relationship we have with cats is tactile, and our pleasure in naming them—or rather, in saying the names they have given themselves—is very much like the pleasure we feel when we pet them. A name is akin to a caress. ("Language is a skin," Roland Barthes writes in *A Lover's Discourse.* "It is as if I had words instead of fingers, or fingers at the tip of my words.") And so a long-term relationship requires that names be continually reinvented.

My Siamese, the cat with whom I share the most passionate attachment, was raised by people who called her Baby and cried when I carried her away, and so even though I would never stoop to calling a *lover* baby, I thought it would be bad luck to change her name. Instead, I shortened it. To B. Teased it out to BeeBee. Beezer. Beemer. Beemeister. Beezermacher. Showering her with syllables like a potentate lavishing jewels on his favorite courtesan.

When I was sick I called her Nurse Applehead. And Barney the Barnacle because she became so clingy when I brought home a new kitten. (His name was Truman, because he was a tiny genius, but he looked so much like a Mouse that everyone called him that—Hairy Hiss Truman when he learned a new growly word.) Meanwhile, Barney the Barnacle begat Barney, Barney Google, Barnes, and, briefly, Noble Barnes. Then one day Baby became Peg. I had an aunt by that name. She was a lesbian; we called her Uncle Peg.

If a family name is a kind of wish about the future of the family, isn't it imaginable that any name can be a kind of wish? And if we name even animals that have no respect for the conventions of obedience, doesn't it make perfect sense that we name vehicles, as if they, too, could know our wishes?

For a while, all my cars had wings, like the Songbird, an old beige Saab named after Sky

King's plane because the first time I dropped acid and drove, I had to straddle the white lines on the thruway and pretend I was coming in for a landing. I would never have made it in a mere automobile. Then there was Fly by Night, an unmuzzled $500 Firebird convertible that my lover and I could barely afford. And Angel, a blue Prelude, purchased with severance pay—and shortly after being ejected from the longest (and worst) relationship I ever had. Go figure: I would never have stuck with a lemon for seven years.

The Toyota Paseo ad reads: "Stylish. Responsive. Fun. If it were a man, you'd marry it." Indeed. Next came Petey (aka Elvis), a black BMW 4x4 with the muscular flanks of a quarter horse, then Tommy Moe, the sturdy, snow-hammering Jeep. The motorcycle I learned on was named after Malcolm Forbes because *he* started riding at fifty. But Malcolm didn't last. When my girlfriend let me ride her fuck-you machine, I ran out and got a bike just like it. We christened them Thelma and Louise, and began harassing taxis. So much for me and marriage.

My mountain bike's name is Spike the Bike because when I ride it, my friend Lane says, I look like the movie gremlin. My road bike became Kiki Whippet after I saw a beautiful greyhound with the same brindle coat when I was out training for the AIDS Ride. Shall I go on? Where does it end? Where does the lover draw the line if not at inanimate objects? Objects that are purely utilitarian, perhaps? I haven't named my desk chair yet, but neither have I named my skis, or my bed, both of which I find more interesting on every level.

If love is an act of faith in our connection, and names are the totem of that faith, a name requires a certain kind of relationship. Some trust that our mutual welfare is a mutual priority. (I've had fewer bomb messages since I named my hard drive Dante, which leads me to believe that if the Unabomber had been able to love anyone, he would not have found technology so off-putting.)

Indeed, love, and naming, both demand *le mot juste* out of respect for the other's otherness.

Why is it, then, that about three weeks into your typical lesbian affair, the two people both become known by the generic "honey"?

Or is that what's meant by the love that dare not speak its name?

---

Tracy Young has written for many national magazines. Her essay "A Few (More) Words About Breasts" won an Honorable Mention in *The Best Essays of 1993*, but her pet assignment was naming beauty products for Ultima II.

LESLIE FEINBERG AND
MINNIE BRUCE PRATT

When I came into the bar in drag, kind of
hunched over, they told me, "Be proud of what
you are," and then they adjusted my tie sort of
like you did. I was like them, they knew I didn't
have a choice. So I never fought them with my
fists. We clapped each other on the back in the bars
and watched each other's backs at the factory.

But then there were the times our real enemies
came in the front door: drunken gangs of sailors,
Klan-type thugs, sociopaths and cops. You always knew when they walked in because someone thought to pull the plug on the jukebox. No
matter how many times it happened, we all still
went "Aw . . ." when the music stopped and then
realized it was time to get down to business.

When the bigots came in it was time to fight,
and fight we did. Fought hard—femme and
butch, women and men together.

If the music stopped and it was the cops at the

door, someone plugged the music back in and we switched dance partners. Us in our suits and ties paired off with our drag queen sisters in their dresses and pumps. Hard to remember that it was illegal then for two women or two men to sway to music together. When the music ended, the butches bowed, our femme partners curtsied, and we returned to our seats, our lovers, and our drinks to await our fates.

That's when I remember your hand on my belt, up under my suit jacket. That's where your hand stayed the whole time the cops were there. "Take it easy, honey. Stay with me baby, cool off," you'd be cooing in my ear like a special lover's song sung to warriors who need to pick and choose their battles in order to survive.

## SUGAR TIT

You say, "I've wondered how you'd explain what it's like to be lovers with someone seen as woman and man." I think of the dance we went to at a friend's house, the whisper about you repeated to me, "Well, it must be a woman, it's with you. But she's wearing men's pants and men's shoes." I don't point out to the whisperer that I am the only woman at the party wearing a skirt. Of the other women, all with short hair and jeans and slacks, some are femmes, some butches with their legs spread apart and their hands in their pockets, some are kiki or androgynous. But no one pushes masculine and feminine to the edge of woman as we do.

Later you say to me, "You gave me everything in front of them." How they stared as you pulled me to you, hand in the small of my back as we danced, your thigh between mine, grinding gently. Your grip on me inexorable and sure, my counterpoint crossing you with my hips. How you began to sweat with desire, and the effort of working against my desire, your arms and legs the channel I flowed between, surging like a river released from underground. You held me as we danced, your shirt wringing wet, and the other women stared at us sliding in and out of womanhood. My skirt swung around my hips. The last man I'd danced with was my husband, whose hands longed for me to hold him like a mother. The last woman I'd danced with wanted me to follow, but her hands weren't strong enough to hold me. You know that when you hold me, I will follow. You know I will give you my breast, but not as sugar tit. You long to see how much pleasure I will let flow through my nipples like milk, gushing and falling on the ground, perhaps in your mouth, perhaps on my own hands for me to lick off.

Did I survive? I guess I did. But only because I knew I might get home to you.

They let us out last, one at a time, on Monday morning. No charges. Too late to call in sick to work, no money, hitchhiking, crossing the border on foot, rumpled clothes, bloody, needing a shower, hurt, scared.

I knew you'd be home if I could get there.

You ran a bath for me with sweet-smelling bubbles. You laid out a fresh pair of white BVDs and a T-shirt for me and left me alone to wash off the first layer of shame.

I remember, it was always the same. I would put on the briefs, and then I'd just get the T-shirt over my head and you would find some reason to come into the bathroom, to get something or put something away. In a glance you would memorize the wounds on my body like a road map—the gashes, bruises, cigarette burns.

Later, in bed, you held me gently, caressing me everywhere, the tenderest touches reserved for the places I was hurt, knowing each and every sore place—inside and out. You didn't flirt with me right away, knowing I wasn't confident enough to feel sexy. But slowly you coaxed my pride back out again by showing me how much you wanted me. You knew it would take you weeks again to melt the stone.

## BEARD

In the grainy black-and-white video, a young dyke, with a face smooth as an eggshell, smears lather on her cheeks and neck, draws a razor across her face and throat. She talks to the audience: "I asked a girl to marry me, and she said, 'Girls can't get married to each other.'" The actress strokes away her imaginary beard with another flourish of the blade, and adds, "So I waited to become a man. I got tired of waiting. Waiting gets tiresome."

When you turn your face to kiss me at a certain angle, I am caressed by an edge of roughness, a rasp of hair at your chin's edge, a reminder of why on the street you're sometimes still taken for a man, an edge that reminds me how you lived as one. If you were bearded when we met, would I have let you kiss me? Would you have told me you were a woman? Or a man? What would you have said of who you were? Would the rough hair on your face have brushed against my mouth, made me want to part the soft hair

curled between your legs, made my hands ready
to caress whatever edge of flesh I found there?

When did we get separated in life, sweet warrior
woman? We thought we'd won the war of liber-
ation when we embraced the word *gay*. Then
suddenly there were professors and doctors and
lawyers coming out of the woodwork telling us
that meetings should be run with Robert's Rules
of Order. (Who died and left Robert god?)

They drove us out, made us feel ashamed of
how we looked. They said we were male chau-
vinist pigs, the enemy. It was women's hearts
they broke. We were not hard to send away, we
went quietly.

The plants closed. Something we never could
have imagined.

That's when I began passing as a man. Strange
to be exiled from your own sex to borders that
will never be home.

You were banished too, to another land with
your own sex, and yet forcibly apart from the
women you loved as much as you tried to love
yourself.

For more than twenty years I have lived on
this lonely shore, wondering what became of you.
Did you wash off your Saturday-night makeup
in shame? Did you burn in anger when women

said, "If I wanted a man I'd be with a real one"?

Are you turning tricks today? Are you waiting tables or learning WordPerfect 5.1?

Are you in a lesbian bar looking out of the corner of your eye for the butchest woman in the room? Do the women there talk about Democratic politics and seminars and co-ops? Are you with women who only bleed monthly, on their cycles?

Or are you married in another blue-collar town, lying with an unemployed auto worker who is much more like me than they are, listening for the even breathing of your sleeping children? Do you bind his emotional wounds the way you tried to heal mine?

Do you ever think of me in the cool night?

I've been writing this letter to you for hours. My ribs hurt bad from a recent beating. You know.

I never could have survived this long if I'd never known your love. Yet still I ache with missing you and need you so.

Only you could melt this stone. Are you ever coming back?

The storm has passed now. There is a pink glow of light on the horizon outside my window. I am remembering the nights I fucked you deep and slow until the sky was just this color.

ASHES

You told me you began to cry when you read the
word *ashes* in one of my poems, you didn't know
why. Sitting in this barren hotel room, I dial 2
over and over on the phone to hear my voice-
mail, your message left at ten P.M. At the end,
your voice breaks again and again on the first syl-
lable: "Baby, baby, do you still love me?" Lonely
here, with the loneliness of years, I am reassured
by that one faltering tone. The voice of the stone
breaking open to the streak of crystal. Your sun-
hot streak against the papery skin of my palm. I
have the power to break apart the rock. Fire inside. Wanting you to take me, burn me up, nothing left of me but ashes, potash to the ground.
Wanting you to sift me through your hands, dis-
perse me, gather me up again, handle me, your
hands gritty with me, as all the while you call me
"Treasure. Precious."

---

Minnie Bruce Pratt is the author of *We Say We Love Each
Other*, *Rebellion: Essays 1980–1991*, *Crime Against Nature*,
and *S/HE*. Leslie Feinberg is the author of the novel *Stone
Butch Blues* and *Transgender Warriors: From Joan of Arc to Ru
Paul*.

# love, maybe

AUDRE LORDE

Always
in the middle
of our bloodiest battles
you lay down your arms
like flowering mines

to conqueror me home.

---

Audre Lorde (1934–1992) published five works of prose, including *The Cancer Journals,* and nine volumes of poetry, including *Chosen Poems Old and New* (1992) (in which this poem appears), and her final work, *The Marvelous Arithmetics of Distance.* She received many honors and awards for her work and from 1991 to 1993 was the New York State poet.